A Dari

Reading Practice

air
fair
chair
stair
despair

bare
dare
share
glare
spare

bear
pear
tear
wear
swear

there
where

their

At the bottom of each page of text, some multisyllable words are split up for the reader.

Contents

Vocabulary

- **tearaways** – young people who behave in a wild and reckless manner
- **glare** – a harsh, bright, dazzling light
- **screech** – a harsh, shrill cry
- **flare** – a burning light
- **clambered** – climbed with both hands and feet
- **ensnared** – captured or caught in
- **scooped** – gathered something up in a swift movement

It was time to get going. Mina stared at the gem.
"Where will you take us this time?" she asked it.
The glare of the sun made it hard to see if the
gem was glowing. She rubbed it. It seemed to
be turning red.

glow ing   turn ing

Gold had taken to the air, flying high over the rest of them. Suddenly he began to squawk and flap his wings.

"Where are you looking?" asked Nat, puzzled. "There's nothing up there."

look ing   no thing

But Gold was still looking up. Suddenly Mina was aware of a string of shapes high up above them. The shapes were hidden in the clouds. She gasped. They were standing under a pair of floating islands!

float ing   is lands

The islands were linked by an arching bridge. Mina spotted a rare sight. A massive, hairy bear sat on one of the islands. Tucked into his lair behind him was a tiny red dragon! Mina gasped again. She needed to share this with Nat.

arch ing   mass ive

"It's the red egg," she told him. "It's already hatched. The red dragon is up there on a floating island. How do we reach it?"

Nat grinned as the clouds shifted.

"They are not floating islands, Mina. They are the tops of massive mountains!"

moun tains

Nat was right. They were at the base of a
pair of mountains so big that parts of them
were hidden in the clouds. The tiny dragon
must have flown up to the top of the mountain
and been trapped by the bear. They needed
to get up there, and fast.

The baby dragons were hatching a plan. They teamed up in pairs and hooked their tiny claws into Nat and Mina. They lifted them up into the air! They headed for the first mountain, where the bear could not see them.

hatch ing   head ed

They needed to reach the little red dragon. Nat began to creep across the bridge. Suddenly Blue screeched in despair. What had she seen? Mina gasped. It was an airship, filled with bounty hunters. It was heading their way!

des pair   air ship

Chapter 3: Little Tearaways!

The airship was heading for the bear. It was racing them.

"It's not fair," puffed Mina as they ran up the steep stairs on the bridge. "They are going by air! We can't get there as quickly as they can."

The dragons had a plan to slow down the airship. They flew up into the air and landed on top of it.

A team of angry baby dragons can be a scary thing! They began to tear at the airship with their teeth and claws, ripping holes into it. There was a massive hissing noise as the air began to escape from the balloon!

an gry   scar y   es cape

The hunters wanted to scare off the dragons. They lit a flare that blinded them with a sudden glare of light. The dragons lost their grip on the airship as it lifted up into the air again. The hunters were heading right for the bear's lair!

Luckily Blue was still clinging to the airship. With a massive bite, she ripped a hole in the side of the balloon. The air hissed as the balloon crumpled and dropped – right in the path of the bear! Had he seen them? The hunters scrambled to their feet, not daring to make a sound.

cling ing   crum pled

Chapter 4: Snaring the Bear

The bear stared for a moment... then pounced!
The hunters were so scared they turned and
ran. Nat and Mina ran to grab the ropes from
the broken airship.

bro ken

Mina and Nat knotted the ropes into a snare.
Green clambered up into a tree, taking the snare
with him. The trap was set. Mina snatched up
a flare that one of the hunters had dropped.
She lit the flare and prepared to run.

clam bered   pre pared

Mina ran, waving the flare in the air. The bear chased it, leaving his lair and the little red dragon. As he ran under the tree, Nat and Green dropped the net of ropes. The angry bear was ensnared in the tangles!

en snared   tan gles

The bear was out of the way! The little red dragon was too scared to fly. Mina crept into his empty lair and carefully scooped her up. She made her a swinging chair from the last rope and lowered her gently down to Bain. "Take care of her, Bain!" she yelled. "It's time to get all these babies safely back to their mum!"

emp ty   care full y